# PASSPORT
# ARGENTINA

# Passport To The World

Passport Argentina
Passport Brazil
Passport China
Passport France
Passport Germany
Passport Hong Kong
Passport India
Passport Indonesia
Passport Israel
Passport Italy
Passport Japan
Passport Korea
Passport Mexico
Passport Philippines
Passport Poland
Passport Russia
Passport Singapore
Passport South Africa
Passport Spain
Passport Taiwan
Passport Thailand
Passport United Kingdom
Passport USA
Passport Vietnam

# PASSPORT ARGENTINA

### Your Pocket Guide to Argentine Business, Customs & Etiquette

**Andrea Mandel-Campbell**

## WORLD TRADE PRESS®
*Professional Books for International Trade*

**World Trade Press**
1450 Grant Avenue, Suite 204
Novato, California 94945 USA
Tel: (415) 898-1124; Fax: (415) 898-1080
USA Order Line: (800) 833-8586
http://www.worldtradepress.com
http://www.globalroadwarrior.com
E-mail: worldpress@aol.com
"Passport to the World" concept: Edward G. Hinkelman
Cover design: Peter Jones, Marge Stewart
Desktop publishing: Joe Reif
Illustrations: Tom Watson
Editor: Jeffrey Edmund Curry

**Copyright Notice**

**Disclaimer**

This publication is designed to provide general information
concerning the cultural aspects of doing business with people from a particular country. It is sold with the understanding that the publisher is not engaged in rendering legal or
any other professional services. If legal advice or other
expert assistance is required, the services of a competent
professional person should be sought.

**Library of Congress Cataloging-in-Publication Data**

Campbell, Andrea, 1969–
Passport Argentina: Your Pocket Guide to Argentine Business,
Customs & Etiquette / Andrea Campbell.
p. cm. -- (Passport to the World)
Includes bibliographical references (p. ).
ISBN 1-885073-21-6
1. Business etiquette--Argentina. 2. Corporate culture--Argentina.
Negotiation in business--Argentina. 4. Industrial management--
Social aspects--Argentina. I. Title. II. Series.
HF5389.3.A7C36  1999
390' .00982--dc21                                          99–16124
                                                                CIP

Printed in the United States of America

# Table of Contents

# Argentina

### *The Silver Republic*

## Overview

## Business Environment

## Customs & Etiquette

## Additional Information

# Argentina
# Quick Look

| | |
|---|---|
| **Official name** | Argentine Republic |
| **Land area** | 2,766,889 sq km |
| **Capital & largest city** | Buenos Aires |
| | 2.96 million |
| **Elevations** | Highest– |
| | Cerro Aconcagua 6.959 m |
| | Lowest–Peninsula Valdés |
| | 48 m below sea level |

**People**

| | |
|---|---|
| Population (1997) | 35.2 million |
| Density | 11.7 persons per sq km |
| Distribution | 86.9% urban, 13.1% rural |
| Annual growth (1989-94) | 1.3% |
| Official language | Spanish |
| Major religions | Roman Catholic, Protestant, Jewish |

**Economy(1997)**

| | |
|---|---|
| GDP | US$322.7 billion |
| | US$8,570 per capita |
| Foreign trade | Imports–US$30.3 billion |
| | Exports–US$25.4 billion |
| Principal trade partners | Brazil 19%, US 13.6%. Chile 5%, Italy 4.6%, Germany 4% |
| Currency | Peso (1AP=100 centavos) |
| Exchange rate | 1AP = US$1 |

**Education and health**

| | |
|---|---|
| Literacy | 96.2% |
| Life expectancy | Women–78.3 years |
| | Men–70.9 years |
| Infant mortality | 19 per 1,000 live births |

# ARGENTINA

## 1 Country Facts

### Geography and Demographics

As the second largest country in South America, Argentina is bordered by Brazil, Paraguay, Uruguay, Bolivia, and Chile. The Andes mountain range lies to the west while the Atlantic Ocean serves as the country's eastern frontier. Argentina's terrain varies widely from arid steppe in the south and high altitude plains or *Altiplano* in the northwest, to jungles and vast floodplains in the northeast; the sprawling grasslands, known as the Pampas, envelop the heart of the country. A country of extremes, Argentina boasts the continent's highest peak, Cerro Aconcagua, reaching an altitude of 6,900 meters (22,834 feet), and its lowest depression, Valdés Peninsula, at 48 meters (157 feet) below sea level.

Despite its indigenous roots, Argentina is largely populated by immigrants of European origin. Spanish Conquistadors first laid claim to the vast plains in the early 16th century. Subsequent large-scale migrations of Spaniards and Italians transformed the capital of Buenos Aires into an almost exclusively European metropolis. At the height of the influx, between 1837 and 1939, more than four million immigrants arrived on Argentine shores. A small but determined British community remains, including vestiges of Welsh settlements dating from the turn of the century, in the southern region known as Patagonia.

Many middle-eastern immigrants, particularly Syrians, Lebanese, and Armenians, also settled, finding the arid north of Argentina similar to their home countries. Koreans now number about 20,000 in Buenos Aires and count among a new wave of immigrants that also includes Eastern Europeans, Peruvians, Bolivians, and Paraguayans.

Away from the capital, the population remains more mestizo, a mix of the indigenous peoples and the *criollo* culture (Argentine-born Spaniards). A few indigenous communities that survived the various conquering campaigns or wars mostly reside in the more isolated northern reaches bordering Chile, Bolivia, and Paraguay and are estimated to number from 100,000 to 300,000 people. The gaucho, Argentina's free-roaming mestizo cowboy of the Pampas, has become the archetype of the Argentine identity. Although no longer free, his nomadic lifestyle has risen to mythological status in poems, music, and art.

## Climate

Argentina's climate is as diverse as its geography, with conditions ranging from muggy tropical in central areas, to dry, desertlike heat in the north, to subarctic freezing at the southern tip of Tierra del Fuego Island. In the southern Patagonian provinces, winds gust much of the year, reaching velocities of 160 kilometers (100 miles) per hour. Temperatures can fall below 0°C (32°F), but the short summers are mild and ideal for traveling.

In the northwest and along much of the Andean pre-cordillera, the climate is dry and desertlike but turns chilly at night. High-border passes to Chile are often closed by snow in the winter. Eastern and central Argentina proves hot and humid in summer. Average summer temperatures hover between 27°C (80°F) and 34°C (94°F) but are often exacerbated by the "heat factor" or humidity, which can push the temperature into the 40°C's (above 100°F). Winters in Buenos Aires, which traditionally dip to 5°C (41°F) and even 0°C (32°F) on the odd occasion (bringing out an abundance of fur coats) have become increasingly temperate. The sun normally shines, except for the occasional semitropical storm, with the average rainfall (900 millimeters/35.4 inches) spread evenly throughout the year.

April, May, October, and November are the best months to travel. And, although Buenos Aires is hot and humid in January and February, roads become traffic free as most locals head off to the beach.

## Business Hours

Most businesspeople arrive at their offices between 9:30 A.M. and 10 A.M., Monday through Friday, and often stay as late as 8 P.M. While schedules are getting tighter in Buenos Aires, many take a two-hour lunch break between 1 and 3 P.M. Many stores also close for siesta, and in the provinces nap-time may last until 4 or 5 P.M. Stores generally stay open from 10 A.M. to 8 P.M., Monday through Friday, but close on Saturdays at 1 P.M. for the rest of the weekend. Shopping centers generally remain open until 10 P.M. everyday except Sunday, when stores close at 5 P.M. *Kioskos* (small corner stores), which sell everything from candy and soft drinks to cigarettes, often remain open all night long.

Banks are generally open from 10 A.M. to 3 P.M., while government offices remain open between 10 A.M. and 5:45 P.M., Monday through Friday.

## National Holidays

New Year's Day . . . . . . . . . . . . . January 1
Good Friday . . . . . . . . . . . . . . March/April
Easter Sunday . . . . . . . . . . . . March/April
Labor Day . . . . . . . . . . . . . . . . May 1
Anniversary of the 1810
Revolution . . . . . . . . . . . . . . . May 25
   Celebrates the revolt against Spanish rule.
Malvinas Day . . . . . . . . . . . . . June 10
   Commemorates the war against Great Britain over the
   Malvinas/Falkland Islands.
Flag Day . . . . . . . . . . . . . . . . . June 20
Independence Day . . . . . . . . . . July 9
Anniversary of the Death
of the Liberator . . . . . . . . . . . August 17
   Marks the death of General José de San Martín, who
   fought against Spanish forces to free much of the conti-
   nent.
Day of the Races . . . . . . . . . . . October 12
   Celebrates the discovery of the Americas in 1492 by
   Christopher Colombus and the integrating of Spanish
   and Indian races.
All Saints' Day . . . . . . . . . . . . . November 1
   Christian feast that honors all the saints.
The Immaculate Conception . . . December 8
Christmas . . . . . . . . . . . . . . . . December 25

## Holidays and Fiestas

Argentines view most holidays as another good reason to have an *asado*—a day-long barbecue in the backyard with friends and family. Each region or province and many towns also celebrate their own special fiesta, which usually relates to a virgin or saintly figure specific to their history. Some of the most well-known figures whose memories are celebrated with annual pilgrimages include the Virgin of Luján in Buenos Aires province and the Virgin of Itatí in Corrientes province.

Better known as *Las Fiestas*, Christmas and New Year's represent the most important holidays of the year. While Christmas usually remains a strictly family affair, friends will visit each other's homes on New Year's Day to wish each other the best for the new year. Day of the Innocents, the equivalent to April Fool's Day, takes place December 29. The festivities continue until January 6, or Day of the Kings, celebrated in remembrance of the three wise men who came to Bethlehem to honor the birth of Jesus. In many homes residents put out water and hay for the wise men's camels while also filling the children's shoes with presents. Carnival, or Mardi Gras, also serves as a children's holiday when unsuspecting passersby are soaked with water balloons.

The Day of the Student or Spring Day is one of Argentina's favorite celebrations. Secondary school students have picnics in the park and give flowers, particularly carnations, as gifts. Many North American holidays are also becoming fashionable. Valentine's Day is gaining in popularity while many Argentines now celebrate Halloween with masquerade parties at home or in discotheques.

## 2     The Argentines

### Colonial Past

From the mid 16th century to the first stirrings of independence in 1810, Argentina was a Spanish colony. The conquistadors christened the estuary running through Buenos Aires the Silver River (*Río de la Plata*) in hopes of finding precious metals, but were disappointed to find nothing in the way of minerals and little else of interest. Administered from the faraway vice-royalty of High Peru in Lima, the tiny settlement was largely a forgotten outpost whose only value lay in its access to the southern Atlantic Ocean, then a little-used trade route. In 1776, Buenos Aires, with a population of 25,000 supported by a bustling trade in contraband and the city's role as a military outpost, became the capital of the sprawling vice-royalty of the Río de la Plata, encompassing Bolivia, Paraguay, Uruguay, and Chile.

Rivalries remained a constant feature between the various settlements in the vast interior, and Buenos Aires, which, fed up with restricted trade under Spanish rule and emboldened by recent victories over the British navy, deposed the reigning viceroy in 1810 on the pretext that the Spanish throne had been usurped by Napoleon. Many of the interior regions raised armies to oppose the Buenos Aires-based revolution, and only in 1816 was independence declared. A pattern of conflict continued for decades, as *caudillos* (strongmen) of the interior squared off against the dominance of the port city in a series of costly civil wars. Finally, in 1862, Buenos Aires established a tenuous hegemony under a federal system.

Several key elements in the following decades would contribute to making Argentina one of the 10 wealthiest countries in the world. Wheat became Argentina's leading export by the turn of the century with the construction of railway links throughout the country, while the invention of refrigerated ship containers was vital to the development of the formerly illegal beef trade. In 1880, under the leadership of General Julio Roca, Argentina's indigenous people were all but eradicated, clearing the land for new pioneering settlements of European immigrants encouraged by the Argentine government to settle in Argentina. The newfound political stability converted Argentina into a true nation-state.

## Golpes De Estado

Argentina's economic golden age in the early 19th century was also marked by a nascent but short-lived move towards democracy. The tradition of rigged elections accorded between various political groups was replaced in 1916 by the first universal vote for all male citizens. But the strong military presence in civilian life, a characteristic of the country's politics until very recently, ended the democratic experiment in 1930 with a coup.

The military regime was soon replaced by bogus governments brought to power through systematic electoral fraud. Champions of the ruling class, the government sought relief from the Great Depression of the 1930s by protecting the large land-owners. The inevitable class friction brought about another coup in 1943 and the election in 1946 of a former labor minister, General Juan Perón, a political ally of the unions and reformist politicians. Perón's ill-fated protectionist policies soon brought the economy to a sputtering halt. In 1955 he was deposed by yet another coup. For the next two decades constitutional governments alternated with military regimes, culminating in 1976 with the country's most infamous and violent dictatorship, dubbed "The Process."

By the early 1980s the repressive regime was in deep economic trouble. In 1982, it sought diversion by invading the Falkland Islands, a British protectorate off the coast of Argentina. The bitter defeat brought the downfall of the dictatorship and a return to democracy. Along with enjoying its longest run of uninterrupted democratic rule, Argentina has made a 180 degree turn in terms of economic policy, shedding state intervention to become not only the most liberal economy in the region, but the most open to foreign investment.

## Big Talkers

If there's one thing Argentines have, it's an opinion. In abundant, smoke-filled cafes rivaling those of Paris, the art of debate carries on unmatched. From the latest controversy in the scandal-ridden life of Argentine soccer great Diego Maradona, to the country's chaotic traffic, and tales of government corruption, Argentines argue all subjects with equal passion and dramatic emphasis.

Politics is among the favorite topics of conversation owing to the country's turbulent history.

Bouts of democracy interspersed with long-running military regimes have left deep political divisions throughout the country. Most Argentines will wear their political affiliations on their sleeve as they would their favorite soccer team.

What Argentines do agree on is where to place blame—on someone else. After running a red light, an Argentine will muster all the indignation humanly possible to somehow disparage the pedestrian he almost killed. Consequently, vocal street altercations are a common occurrence.

But perhaps Argentines find their greatest verbal pleasure in lamenting an unfortunate occurrence in life. As one old Tango saying goes, *El que no llora no mama* (He that doesn't cry is not breast fed). Their chronic sense of malaise has provided rich material for the heart-wrenching lyrics of Tango music, born in the backroom bars of Buenos Aires at the turn of the century before acquiring a worldwide following. It is that same feeling of despair that has provided abundant fodder for psychoanalysis; only Paris can claim more psychiatrists than Buenos Aires. Such analysis is considered integral to one's general state of health and is a standard part of the normal employee benefit package.

## Language

As with most things, Argentines have put a personal stamp on their brand of Italian-accented Spanish. They differ from the rest of South America by replacing the second personal singular *tu* with *vos* and with it the corresponding verb conjunctions. They are perhaps most known for their use of *che* (hey), which earned the Argentine-born leftist guerrilla and Cuban revolutionary the nickname, Ernesto "Che" Guevera.

Argentines have no qualms reinterpreting the

language either. Argentine slang, known as *Lunfardo*, traces its roots to the mass of mostly working class Italian immigrants who came to Argentina at the turn of the century. While some say the language was created to avoid police detection over illegal dealings, Lunfardo soon became the chosen language of Tango music and remains very much alive to this day. Examples of Lunfardo include: *gita*, *mosca*, *mangos*, and *morlacos*, all different expressions for money. A popular Lunfardo word is *mina*, which in regular Spanish means *a mine*, but to Argentines means woman. An official Lunfardo institute dates back to the 1960s, and younger generations continue to add to the numerous Lunfardo dictionaries with sayings such as *Mi viejo saltó como leche hervida*—literally, my old man jumped like boiled milk.

## Pass the Mirror Please

Argentines love to see and be seen. *Porteños*, or the people of the port, as the 12 million inhabitants of Buenos Aires and its surrounding area are called, concern themselves greatly with appearance. Three ingredients exist to looking good in this fairly conformist society: dressing well, a slender body, and a well-toned suntan. *Porteños* dress to the hilt to go to the local neighborhood cafe and burn for hours in the semitropical midday sun to get a proper tan. While no less concerned about weight, dieting is almost a national sport.

Buenos Aires is also a world center for cosmetic surgery. Medical insurance covers everything from nose jobs to tummy-tucks and liposuction. Many blame the popularity of plastic surgery on Argentine President Carlos Menem, under whose administration the cult of beauty has reached new heights. Menem, who enjoys the company of movie stars and sports legends, has himself undergone plastic surgery as has his flamboyant ex-wife. Political observers have noted that Menem's reliance on image was not lost on his colleagues. Since he took over the presidency in 1989, several leading politicians have undergone extreme image changes that included extensive surgery.

## Family

While an increasingly interconnected world holds a visible impact on Argentina's once closed economy, family remains the pillar of society and still demands the highest loyalty. Argentines are protective of their children, respectful of their parents, and usually live within a few blocks of family. All major decisions are first discussed within the family. Most children live at home until they marry, and if they do move out to test their freedom, they often move back home.

Friendship is almost as dear as family, and Argentines consider disappointing a friend as bad as letting down one's own mother. Argentines recognize a favor based purely on friendship as *una gauchada* (a gaucholike gesture of honor). Many maintain that the best business deals are made in front of a table full of good food and good friends.

Family gatherings such as Christmas are sacred, but also large and raucous. An Argentine dedicates Sunday to family and day-long lunches of pasta, *matambre* (pressed stomach lining), and wine. Married couples continue to visit their in-laws for Sunday lunches—usually the wife's parents since mother-daughter relations represent perhaps the strongest link in the family chain. On special occasions, including Independence Day on July 9, families will hold an *asado*—serving a strictly carnivorous fare of beef and lamb roasted over a huge open pit fire in the backyard or in the countryside.

## Religion

Catholicism remains the official religion of Argentina with about 90 percent of its 35 million inhabitants professing to be Catholic, although evangelical Protestants continue to make inroads in the poorer areas of Buenos Aires and the provinces. Although Jews make up just 1 percent of the population, the country's 350,000-strong community is the largest in Latin America and the fourth largest in the world. Many Jews hold high government positions and are some of the closest advisors to President Menem, a Muslim-born Arab of Syrian descent. (He is often referred to as *el turco*—the turk—a common nickname for Arabs, or *el sultan* due to his monarchical tendencies.) Menem converted to Catholicism upon entering politics since only Catholics could hold the office of President until the Constitution was changed in 1994.

The Catholic Church remains powerful in Argentina and its leaders still retain political clout; however, that power has waned significantly in recent years. Only about 20 percent of the population actively practices Catholicism. Many Argentines make the sign of the cross when they pass a church and wear medallions of the Virgin Mary, but more often then not, they accept the religion on their own terms. Although the law makes abortion illegal it is still practiced, as is premarital sex. Unmarried couples living together is a popular trend, and divorce is growing since its controversial legalization in 1987.

## Tolerance, Racism, Extremism

One will often hear Argentines state quite simply, if not without a little pride, that racism doesn't exist in Argentina. As proof, they will point appallingly to examples of intolerance in Europe and North America. For all of its racial diversity, however, Argentina is not without its problems.

Democracy has been punctuated in Argentina with bouts of military dictatorship culminating in the country's so-called Dirty War, which lasted from 1976 to 1983. It is said that during that time, anywhere from 9,000 to 30,000 people "disappeared" when military death squads took to the streets to eliminate political opposition.

It was not the first time extreme measures had been taken regarding the population. In the late 1870s, General Julio Roca led a successful campaign, known as the *Conquest of the Wilderness,* to exterminate marauding Indian tribes from the rolling grasslands of the Pampas. With a history as a former slave market, Buenos Aires was 25 percent black in the 19th century. It remained so until the slaves and their descendants were sent to fight wars as cannon fodder against Argentina's neighbors.

The country's remaining indigenous peoples, the darker skinned *mestizos* or *morochos*, live mostly in the provinces and remain at the bottom of the social ladder. Consequently, Argentina's neighbors, such as Bolivia and Paraguay, are not held in high esteem due to their prevalence of indigenous people. Many of these neighbors have illegally flocked to Argentina to look for work and Argentines have blamed them for increasing crime rates. These illegals often end up living in makeshift shantytowns known as *villa miserias* on Buenos Aires's poorer southern side.

In 1995, the government passed a law requiring immigrants to have a work contract in an effort to stem the tide of an estimated one million illegal immigrants. Recently, several Lower House representatives presented a bill that would financially reward people for reporting illegal immigrants to the authorities.

## Class Friction

Argentina distinguishes itself from many other countries in Latin America by its substantial middle class. The country leads the region in social spending, has a literacy rate of 96 percent, and boasts the highest GDP per capita income (US$8,570) in the region. It is even now a candidate for membership in the Organization for Economic Cooperation and Development (OECD).

Much of the country's egalitarian way is rooted in the arrival of European immigrants who flooded Argentina at the turn of the century just as they had done in North America. A popular saying goes as follows: Mexicans are descended from the Aztecs, Peruvians come from the Incas, and Argentines came off the boats. Many leading Argentine industrialists and entrepreneurs proudly hearken back to their immigrant forefathers' humble beginnings in search of the "American Dream."

## The Rise of Perón

For many blue-collar workers, greater equality with the country's land-owning oligarchy didn't come until the charismatic General Juan Perón and his wife, Eva (Evita), came to power in 1946. Perón forged his populist movement with the support of the working class, recognizing and establishing powerful unions and introducing wide-ranging social benefits while fighting the entrenched power of the *estancieros*, or ranch owners.

Perón's detractors remember him as a ruthless dictator who quashed personal freedoms and modeled his regime after Europe's defeated fascists.

Much of the economic problems, which were to haunt the country for decades after, were also blamed on Perón's interventionist and projectionist policies. Along with high tariffs on imports, taxes on ranch wealth were used to pay for social services and support new, often inefficient industry.

To many, however, Perón's social policy, known as *Justicialismo*, after which the party is named (Partido Justicialista), established social equality and ended the feudal exploitation of what Perón referred to as the *descamisados*, or shirtless ones. As a result, the hegemony of the elite and landed families has largely faded, although hints remain on Argentina's famed polo fields and in plush shopping trips abroad.

Still, Perónism adopted its own brand of nepotism with personal contacts and family ties weighing heavily when it came to getting a job. With the introduction of far-reaching economic reforms in the early 1990s and an accompanying record level of unemployment, the layers of nepotism are slowly shedding. As a result, the once coddled middle class, grown complacent in generous government jobs, suffers along with the lower classes. The gap between rich and poor is starting to widen for the first time in decades as this middle class falls towards the economic bottom.

## Corruption

Buenos Aires, named after the patron saint of "good airs" under Spanish colonial rule, traces its humble economic beginnings to smuggling. The port city, founded by Pedro de Mendoza in 1536 on the muddy waters of the Rio de la Plata estuary, was declared off limits to free trade by its Spanish rulers. The ingenious native Argentines, however, soon found a way around the barrier by establishing a lucrative illicit trade with the Portuguese. They first plundered wild cows for their hides and then arranged for ships loaded with merchandise to dock for "repairs" and illicit bartering.

Centuries later, smuggling of many sorts still exists. In fact, according to polls, Argentines list organized crime and government corruption as their main concern, following unemployment. Beyond that, some 75 percent of Argentines believe high-level government officials are "very corrupt" while the country's police forces provoke similar concern. The police force for the province of Buenos Aires has a particularly bad reputation, with purported links to gambling and money laundering rings, prostitution, and even murder.

## Nationalism

To the chagrin of most Argentines, no such thing as "a true Argentine identity" exists. In fact, 40 percent of Buenos Aires Argentines identify themselves as *Galician* – from Spain, or *Tano* – slang for Italian. Although holding fast to their roots and even their foreign passports, few would dream of living elsewhere.

In fact, according to national mythology, Argentina is the most beautiful country in the world, standing head and shoulders above anything else South America has to offer. An Argentine can describe every part of his beloved country, whether he's been there or not—and any infringement on that land is jealously defended. As a result, several border disputes have erupted with neighboring Chile, and a healthy antagonism has developed between the two countries for what Argentines perceive as Chilean attempts to steal their land.

The same attitude landed Argentina in an ill-fated war with Great Britain in 1982 over the Falkland Islands—known in Argentina as the Islas Malvinas. Argentina's claim to sovereignty over the islands, home to a few thousand kelpers and some sheep, still remains very much alive in the national consciousness. Famed Argentine writer Jorge Luis Borges described the war over the islands as "two bald men fighting over a comb." Yet national holidays mark the event, and highway signs dot the country declaring *Las Malvinas son Argentinas*—the Malvinas are Argentine.

## An Unsavory Recent Past

Argentina is also sadly renowned for serving as a safe haven to some of the most infamous Nazi criminals to escape from Germany after World War II. Under the leadership of General Juan Domingo Perón, many Nazis were housed in government buildings and provided with new identities. Even today, neo-Nazis, some being direct descendants of the real thing, periodically desecrate Jewish cemeteries and bomb Jewish community centers. There is even evidence of membership by some of Argentina's security forces.

## Argentina versus South America

Argentines believe the physical location of their country in South America is merely a geographical accident of fate. Buenos Aires is commonly known as the Paris of South America and its inhabitants are described as Spaniards who talk like Italians, dress like Frenchmen, and think they're British.

As such, Argentines, particularly those from the capital city, believe they are the most educated, sophisticated, and cultured people around. For them, the Argentine-born General José de San Martin liberated most of South America from colonial

rule, while writers Jorge Luis Borges, Ernesto
Sábato, Julio Cortázar, and Osvaldo Soriano have
no peers on the continent.

Home to the poignant accordion melodies of
Tango music, Argentina also boasts traditional folk-
loric singers like Mercedes Sosa and Althahualpa
Yupanqui and rocker Charly Garcia. Its painters
have also received critical acclaim, with Antonio
Berni and Florencio Molina Campos topping the
list. And when it comes to the most sacred and
beloved *futbol* (soccer) there is the unforgettable
Diego Maradona. Other sports greats include race
car hero Juan Manuel Fangio and tennis star Gabri-
ela Sabatini.

But as easily as Argentines primp and preen,
they will just as readily bemoan the behavior of
their fellow Argentines and the state of their society
in general. They complain that no one respects the
law, nobody pays taxes (including the complainer),
and everybody in the government is a thief. Only
Argentines, however, are qualified to complain
about Argentina. Their self-important attitude has
made them a favorite source of material for jokes in
the rest of Latin America. As one popular jest goes
(often told by Porteños themselves): *What's the best
deal going in Argentina?—Buy a Porteño for what he's
worth and sell him for what he says he's worth.*

Argentina's physical isolation at the tip of the
Southern Cone has, nonetheless, made Argentines
keenly curious about what others think of them.
With Europe and North America considered cultural leaders, Argentines are particularly interested
to know how developed Western countries view
them. Newspaper articles written about Argentina
in Europe and the United States will often make the
front pages in Buenos Aires.

## 3 Cultural Stereotypes

While Argentines are basically divided between those who live in Buenos Aires and those who live in the provinces, some stereotypes are nationwide.

### Arrogant

*Argentines are rude, vain, and superficial.*

Argentines, particularly Porteños, have managed to garner the general disdain of most Latin American countries due to their often superior behavior. According to Argentines, however, their Latin neighbors are merely jealous.

Their fondness for cellular phones, expensive clothes, and showy jewelry proves most prevalent in the affluent Buenos Aires neighborhood of Barrio Norte. In fact, Porteños carry a more unpopular reputation in the provinces of Argentina than they do abroad. Argentines of the interior, well-known for their hospitality and warmth, have long felt disgruntled by the preeminent position the capital city has held in the history of the country. As far as many Porteños are concerned, however, Buenos Aires represents Argentina, and the provincial inhabitants count only as *cabecitas negras* (little black heads).

## On the Sly Rather Than the Straight and Narrow

*Argentines have an affinity for shady dealings and a
distinct aversion to following rules.*

According to the rules of the *viveza criolla*, or
native cunning used to swindle others, if you get
duped, it's your own fault. This not unlike the caveat
emptor (let the buyer beware) attitude in many
developed economies.

When it comes to business, Argentines do not
necessarily give straightforward answers. Backroom
deals, kickbacks, and *coimas* (bribes) are not an
uncommon part of the bargain and are dubbed *nego-
ciados* (dirty dealings). Organized crime, known as
the mafia, remains alive and well in Argentina.

After years of economic isolation, however,
recently introduced market reforms are changing
attitudes. Society increasingly has pressured the
government to clean up its act. Meanwhile, the government has increased the pressure on its citizens to
cough up millions lost annually to tax evasion.

Nonetheless, Argentines' almost innate dislike
for rules isn't expected to change in the near future.
The attitude described as *piola*, particularly developed
in Buenos Aires, is perhaps best explained by traffic
practices. Many Argentines consider red traffic lights
optional and wouldn't hesitate to drive down a street
the wrong way if it proves more convenient.

## Siesta Time

*Argentines are slackers and lack a strong work ethic.*

Argentines generally regard work as a means of
survival rather than a way to get ahead in the world.
One will rarely find an Argentine businessperson in
his office before 10 A.M., and an appointment made
prior to that may possess good intentions but will
rarely produce the individual. Argentines tend to

work later—often until 8 P.M., but an attempt to reach them during their two-hour lunch between 1 and 3 P.M. will likely prove unsuccessful. (In the provinces, afternoon naps are still taken between 1 and 4 P.M.). The nighttime lifestyle and midday heat offer good reasons for an afternoon nap.

The tradition of drinking *mate* has also contributed to the Argentines' unhurried approach to life. An herb drunk from a hollowed-out squash gourd, mate is not only a time-honored but a very time-consuming tradition. Shared among a group, each person sips the warm, green liquid until it is finished. The gourd is refilled and passed on to the next person. Many Argentine companies have recently decided to prohibit drinking mate at the office because of its effect on productivity.

Nonetheless, Argentina's greatest mate drinkers are perhaps its hardest workers. The Argentine cowboy, or the gaucho, is highly respected as a tireless, hardy, leather-worn worker who rises before dawn and often travels hundreds of miles on horseback to survey migrating cattle herds and the sprawling farms of the Pampas. With the help of the gaucho, Argentina became one of the world's ten richest countries at the turn of the century, in its role as the world's breadbasket.

# 4   Regional Differences

As Juan Batista Alberdi, the 19th-century Argentine intellectual noted, Argentina is really two countries—Buenos Aires and the Interior. Since Argentina's colonial beginnings as the Viceroyalty of The River Plate under the Spanish Empire in 1776, its rulers granted the port city the authority to collect customs fees. The port guarded these rights jealously, creating resentment among the poorer provinces. The schism deepened after Buenos Aires political leaders revolted against Spanish rule on May 25, 1810, and the two sides squared off under opposing political currents that would result in 50 years of civil war.

The Unitarians, largely Frenchified port dwellers, looked to concentrate power in the city and argued for an exclusive democracy lead by local enlightened men. The Federalists, represented by provincial *caudillos*, or strongmen, and supported by gaucho armies, wanted provincial autonomy and a relationship based on mutual consent. Distrust of Buenos Aires continued to grow as the city aspired to control the interior. It did so, at the expense of the provinces, by usurping profits through customs taxes and insisting all trade pass through the port.

To this day, enmity exists on economic, political, and racial fronts. As one well-known saying goes, *God is everywhere, but attends church in Buenos Aires.* The traditionally working class Partido Justicialista, or Perónists, for example, have never been elected in the more well-to-do federal capital. Porteños often refer to the current Perónist President, Carlos Saul Menem, a modern-day caudillo from the northern province of La Rioja, as *Mendez*—a veritable snub of the president along with his provincial and political roots. Such a reference also serves to assist in avoiding *mufa*, or bad luck. However, due to such snobbery, a foreign traveler will often receive better treatment than a *Porteño* when both are traveling in the provinces.

## Dialects and Foreign Tongues

Regionalism remains strong in Argentina due to immigration patterns. Northern Argentina is "more like Bolivia," say many Buenos Aires inhabitants, due to the large indigenous presence and cross-border movement from Bolivia and Paraguay. Many indigenous communities still live in the area, including the Colla, Wichí, and Chorote people. Many gauchos, who are usually a mestizo mix, often speak Guaraní, one of the two officials languages of Paraguay and the language of the Guaraní people. Tribes of Tehuelche and Mapuche live in the southern provinces.

Near the southern end of the Andes range, one can hear German, and at the southern coast, Welsh, by settlers who traveled to Argentina to preserve their language. Many Argentines, particularly in Buenos Aires, also speak English as well as French and Italian. As one moves into the provinces, European languages become less commonly heard.

# 5 Government & Business

Over much of this century, Argentine governments, varying from military to populist rule, have promoted economic isolation. Under Perón, the government largely nationalized foreign-owned industries while implementing state subsidies for inefficient manufacturers in an effort to make Argentina self-sufficient. Destructive import substitution policies heavily sapped Argentina's agriculture, its greatest natural resource. The Instituto Argentino de Promocion de Intercambio, a state monopoly set up under Perón, bought agricultural commodities from domestic producers, paying one-third to one-quarter of international prices, which were later sold for large profits on the international market to support the welfare state. At the same time, the government prohibited the importation of many consumer goods in a bid to promote local production.

But much has changed. Argentina has taken a 180 degree turn, embracing the most liberal economic policy in the region. Foreign investors have returned to Argentina in droves, attracted by a veritable fire sale on state-owned industries and the removal of prohibitive investment laws. The country's GDP grew by 51 percent between 1990 and

1997, prompting Argentina to become an international favorite for direct foreign investment.

## Privatization

The turning point for Argentina came in 1991 when the Argentine peso was pegged to the U.S. dollar under the now famous *Convertability Plan.* The move marked the "rebirth of Argentina" by putting an end to debilitating hyperinflation which had reached heights of 5000 percent a year in the late 1980s. Aside from creating a stable economic environment in which to invest, the Argentine government, under President Carlos Menem, took a decidedly hands-off approach to the economy by undertaking the most thorough privatization of state-owned companies on the continent.

To date, the government has collected upward of US$30 billion by selling or granting concessions—often under dubious legal circumstances—for everything from the national mail service and the country's airports, to the flagship airline (Aerolineas Argentinas) and the Buenos Aires zoo. The auction of state-owned industry, the largest purveyor of the country's hidden unemployment, lead to heavy job losses. In the most dramatic case, Y.P.F., an oil company, cut its head count from 50,000 to 7,500 following privatization. As a result, periodic protests arise from the country's disaffected middle-class and blue-collar workers, many of whom enjoyed the perks of working for state companies. Argentines use the term *ñoquis,* a potato pasta served on the 29th of every month, as a pun referring to its synonym *no aqui* (not here) for government employees who suddenly materialize at the end of the month to pick up their paychecks.

## The 1994 Constitution

Argentina's new constitution, which gave President Menem the right to run for re-election in exchange for certain concessions to the opposition, also granted the provinces their long-awaited autonomy. Public institutions like the education system passed from federal to provincial control. In many cases, however, it has caused more confusion. Federal laws, which have national jurisdiction, may or may not apply in certain provinces, depending on whether that province decides to pass its own law on the matter. Such obstacles have been faced by newly enacted environmental legislation and a 1993 mining legislation, since provinces are now considered the owners of their natural resources.

## The Second Reform of the State

After deregulating, decentralizing, and privatizing in 1990 and 1991, the government has embarked on an ambitious plan to make public administration and public institutions more efficient. The government has eliminated 17 secretariats, 39 subsecretariats, 4,600 positions, and 500 contracts under the plan, christened the Second Reform of the State. Big restructuring challenges remain in the area of health, education, and the justice system. Social spending has come under particularly heavy scrutiny. While Argentina spends more on social programs than any other country in Latin America, transparency and dispersal are problems. Currently 30 percent of all funds never reach their destination.

Similarly, the Justice system has been heavily criticized for its lack of independence. A widely held belief asserts that five of the nine Supreme

Court judges answer directly to President Menem, who in fact appointed them. Under the 1994 Constitution, a Council of the Magistrate was to be established. As one of the concessions afforded the opposition Unión Civica Radical party that paved the way for Menem's re-election, the institution would carry out the independent appointment as well as removal of judges. Established only recently after much delay, it is still uncertain how effective the council will be.

## Mercosur

The customs union forged in 1995, representing Argentina, Brazil, Paraguay, and Uruguay, has helped to dynamize trade in the region. The four-country bloc which boasts an aggregate GDP of US$900 billion and a population of 200 million, continues to attract new members and foreign investment interest. Most recently Chile and Bolivia have signed on as free trade partners, with the Andean Pact countries of Columbia, Venezuela, Ecuador, and Peru next on the list in anticipation of hemispheric free trade plans in 2005. The bloc has also begun negotiations with the European Union to establish a free trade agreement.

From outside, The Southern Common Market (Mercosur), has been accused of protectionist policies, particularly in regards to its car regime, which allows for free trade of automobiles and parts between Argentina and Brazil. As a result of the closer ties, Argentina sells one-third of its exports to Brazil, a situation that many consider precarious considering the region's emerging market profile, and recent market volatility. Government and business are now trying to boost Argentine exports (which remain poor, representing just 9 percent of GDP compared to a regional average of 15 percent) outside the region, with sales of fresh beef to the United States and wine to Europe, Asia, and North America.

## Regulated Retail

The unrestricted boom of hypermarkets (large, mass-oriented retail stores) in recent years has managed to put many smaller shopkeepers out of business. As a result, the province of Buenos Aires has been the first to pass a law limiting their growth. Hypermarkets may not surpass 2,500 square meters, and developers must provide a socio-economic study of the impact to the public before construction is approved.

## Red Tape

Despite Argentina's newly liberalized profile, it remains a highly litigious country and government red tape can prove a bureaucratic nightmare. Nonetheless, government has made some efforts to streamline. While legal cases can take years to drag through the courts, the government has introduced obligatory mediation and optional arbitration in an effort to resolve economic-related disputes before they reach the courts. The introduction of a privatized preshipment inspection service for imports along with the separate treatment of commercial and personal goods have combined to make the onerous customs system more efficient.

# The Work Environment

### Out with the Old

The old land-owning families that used to rule Argentina at the turn of the century "are ruined," says a member of one of the handful of original bank and land-owning clans. Replaced by what is being dubbed the *noblesa mediatica* or media nobility, these *nuevos ricos* (newly wealthy) have made the bulk of their fortunes following the liberalization of the Argentine economy in the early 1990s. The Argentine press has subsequently raised them to near star status. "You don't exist if you're not in the media," says a member of Buenos Aires society. As a result, one public relations executive tells of a client who bought ten pages of magazine space to write about himself.

As is true in many cultures, it is often difficult to be considered for a business deal or get through the phalanx of secretaries that usually surround most company directors without connections. Their attitude is "Who are you to be calling me?" says a specialist in company liaisons. "You have to have a high profile, you have to be known, and you have to have money." This is a familiar refrain in emerging markets.

Still, there does exist a healthy respect for the self-made man. But it is "even better if you come from a well-known family," notes a Porteño executive.

## A Rigid Labor Force

Double-digit unemployment has been the main fallout from the recent liberal economic reforms. While consistent growth has helped to ease the pain, reform of Argentina's rigid labor market is key to alleviating the problem in the long run, say leading economists. As it stands, the majority of labor contracts still date from 1975 and the central union retains the right to negotiate any new contract, even for a small green grocer in a provincial town. Many sectoral unions also enjoy expansive benefits, which include receiving a percentage of all product sales or a share of the interest made on all bank accounts. Added to this are employer-paid benefits representing an additional 33 percent on top of take-home salary. Indemnities for being fired are also prohibitively high and have prevented many smaller companies from shedding unnecessary personnel and modernizing equipment.

Close to full employment exists for university graduates, but the country faces structural unemployment for unskilled people, particularly with younger and older workers. In the provinces the problem is exacerbated since many refuse to move despite the shutdown of government-run industries. In many provinces new projects are approved on the condition they hire locally.

## Not in the Job Description

With such a rigid labor system, companies find

it difficult to get workers to perform tasks not specifically outlined in their job descriptions. Duties can be extremely particular; for example, Argentine companies employ people just to serve coffee to other employees. The large amount of bureaucracy and the technological backwardness that Argentina suffered from for years made paying a bill a day-long odyssey. As a result, companies invented a whole new job category known as *cadetes*—people whose duty it is to stand in line. However, even with such exacting job descriptions, responsibilities still remain open to interpretation by union leaders, making teamwork a difficult concept to achieve.

Newer industries or interests that have entered the Argentine market in recent years since economic reform will find they have an easier platform on which to work. Many car manufacturers who have set up in Argentina to benefit from a shared free trade regime with Brazil, are large and powerful enough to write their own labor agreements. This often includes more flexibility in job descriptions.

## Top-Heavy Decisions

Surveying some of Argentina's largest companies, one will discover (and many Argentines will lament) that owners are mostly foreign. Nonetheless, some of the country's most powerful conglomerates remain private, family-run affairs. As a result, these family-run companies tend to exhibit a more rigid and hierarchical structure than their North American or European counterparts.

Decisions are made at the top. Managers tend not to delegate, nor do they keep lower-level employees informed about decisions. A mid-level manager working for one of Argentina's most powerful companies with annual sales of $2 billion complained that decision making was left up to just three people. With so much on an executive's plate, decisions take time to materialize and must then still pass through a lengthy implementation process.

At the same time, many Argentines consider taking orders from someone else to be undignified and weak, preferring to give orders rather than take them. Nevertheless, despite an aversion for receiving instruction, employees will avoid open conflict or direct opposition with superiors.

## Money as an End in Itself

An Argentine's work ethic is quite similar to the one espoused by most Americans, Germans, or Hong Kong Chinese who view money as an end in itself. While Argentines do work until all hours and a few define themselves by their careers, there is *mucha franella*—a lot of time wasted. "In Argentina, people want to be famous and have a lot of money, but they just don't want to work hard for it," says one executive.

But notions have begun to change to a degree, especially among the young. Many have embraced the competition of an open economy. As a result, plenty of hard-working and committed individuals are eager for new opportunities and challenges. But while serious about their work, they retain a relaxed and friendly approach to business.

# Women in Business

### The Legend of "Evita"

Eva Duarte de Perón represents Argentina's first true icon of female power. A poor actress from the provinces, "Evita" (little Eva) married General Juan Perón and ruled as veritable copresident until she died in 1952 of uterine cancer at the age of 33. A controversial figure to this day in Argentina, her memory carries a love-hate relationship. Responsible for turning her husband's following into more of a religion than a political movement, she supported the trade unions, dedicated herself to the poor, and mocked the aristocratic class, all the while remaining an Argentine fashion queen.

Millions gathered to hear her speak and her biography, *La Razon de Mi Vida*, was proscribed reading in Argentine schools for years. She also lobbied for female inclusion in politics, and in 1947, under Eva's rule, Argentina gave the vote to women. Current President Carlos Menem called her, "the architect of women's daily lives for the past 50 years."

While much about her life remains clouded in mystery and political propaganda, her early death contributed to a saintly, almost unearthly mystique. Like a saint, her body was embalmed and put on state exhibition. After armed forces held her body for years, she was eventually buried in an unmarked grave in Milan for safety. Eva's remains were returned to Argentina in 1973 when her husband came out of exile in Spain. Her grave, located in the elite cemetery of La Recoleta in Buenos Aires, became a place of pilgrimage for her admirers who keep the vault adorned with flowers.

## Semi-Queen or Semi-Saint

Ironically, the women that have entered politics after Evita have shared a similar legacy, described by some feminists as the "semi-queen or semi-saint" condition. A 1991 law that mandates that women hold a minimum of 30 percent of the congressional seats has resulted in many women being elected primarily for pasts marked by personal tragedy. Graciela Fernandez Meijide, Argentina's most popular politician, (described by President Menem as only good for a housewife) lost a son during the military dictatorship. Similarly, Marta Oyhanarte, a municipal counselor, lost her husband when he was kidnapped and killed by leftist guerrillas. Another political force, The Mothers of the Plaza de Mayo, have gained international recognition for their weekly protest before Congress demanding to know the whereabouts of their "disappeared" sons and daughters.

This martyr effect carries over into the commercial community. Ernestina Herrera de Noble, owner of the multimedia corporation, Grupo Clarín, and the flamboyant owner of an industrial conglomerate, Amalia de Fortabat, are both widows who have successfully managed to build on their husbands' impressive holdings. Their affluent lifestyles have made them leading members of Argentine society's unofficial royalty.

## Work

Women make up 40 percent of the workforce, and in the greater Buenos Aires area one out of three preside as head of a household. Nonetheless, women earn an average of 30 to 40 percent less than their male colleagues. Their careers remain mostly in low-paying, traditionally female-dominated areas including social services, teaching, and domestic work.

Still, women represent 60 percent of the student body at the respected University of Buenos Aires. Less likely to get jobs when they graduate, (only 6 percent currently reaching managerial positions), a growing number of women garner respect for succeeding in business despite the odds. "Women can get to the top—it's just not easy," said one female executive. "But she'll still be expected to fill in for the secretary if there's no other woman to answer the phones."

True, some men simply refuse to deal with women in business, whether employers or clients. Most women, however, are not defined by their career, often quitting once they get married. If a women does decide to remain on the job, the state provides three months of maternity leave as well as child subsidies, and companies are obliged to provide day care. Abortion is illegal and an estimated 400 women a year die attempting amateur abortion operations.

## Machismo is Alive and Well

*You are like an angel that has fallen from heaven* goes one of the more poetic come-ons, or *piropos*, a woman is likely to hear among the whistles and throaty whispers on the street. Argentine women consider the attention a compliment that is par for the course alongside the well-mannered *caballeros*—or gentlemen—who open doors and always wait for a woman to leave an elevator first before exiting. In the office, respectful flirting is "part of the game" and a woman's civil status always stands as the object of immediate and intense interest. Although expected to dress provocatively, an Argentine woman operates on a look-but-don't-touch mentality.

Although machismo is alive and well in Argentina, it is rivaled by a local brand of female chauvinism. Driven by fierce competition, a "woman will X-ray every single woman she passes in the street," says one housewife. Women consider counterparts who aren't married by their 30's as desperate and, as such, a definite threat. Many women consider the high value placed on looks, including a trademark slenderness and tight clothes, a prerequisite, which men also appreciate. However, a female executive states with no sense of irony, "We don't dress for men, we dress for other women."

## Serve with Reserve

Although expected to show femininity in their dress, the business world does not take seriously those who wear overly provocative clothes or are too pretty. An Argentine woman must strike a fine balance if she seeks acceptance. That means dressing elegantly, preferably not smoking or drinking, and choosing her words carefully.

Although the same rules don't apply for foreign women, Argentine females must take care not to challenge men directly or negotiate too aggressively. "If you do, it can ruin a deal," said one cosmetics executive. A woman must know her place and behave in a reserved manner. "What little you say has to be right on the money," says another business woman. "You have to give him time to show you aren't competing against him." Argentine men feel particularly uncomfortable with a woman paying for a meal, even if she has invited. To avoid an awkward moment, it is best to warn the restaurant in advance not to bring the bill to the table.

## 8  Making Connections

### Personal Relationships

Personal relations mean everything to an Argentine. Friendships often date back to secondary or even primary school. In fact, doing a favor for a friend is called a *gauchada*, a gaucholike act of kindness. A source of pride, this selfless gesture allows an Argentine to express his concern for others. Be aware that there is a great deal of reciprocity implied. Even foreigners will be expected to return a favor in the future.

But while ties often date back to childhood, relations are likely conditioned by some kind of shared ideology. Whether a religion, philosophy, ethnic group, or a political affiliation, Argentines tend to relate most things in their lives to a certain value system. In older generations and the military, for example, the Catholic Church remains a strong identifying force. Other than ethnic roots, political affiliation stands among the most notable of unifying factors. Similarly, a strong left-leaning ideological current, rooted in the rejection of perceived U.S. imperialism in decades past, still finds many adherents today. For this reason, most Argentines immediately identify themselves as belonging to one particular political grouping or another.

Nonetheless, they remain very open to new people and ideas, particularly from Western developed countries. Argentines are quick to recognize the latest trends in fashion and technology. Many have studied abroad in Europe and the United States to acquire a sophisticated world view.

## Finding an "Enchufado"

Even if the head of a company expresses interest in meeting with a foreign colleague, getting past his secretary is virtually impossible without some kind of inside track. The key may simply rest in your ability to say you are calling *de parte de,* on behalf of, someone he knows. More than likely, however, you will need to contact an *enchufado*—an individual who has high-level connections in your industry segment.

Your bank, embassy, local business organizations, or even common friends and acquaintances may be able to direct you toward an *enchufado*. Many public relations firms also dedicate themselves to introducing businesspeople and acting as an intermediaries. For a meeting with government officials, you'll need to do the same. While some newly created ministries, such as the mining secretariat, respond quickly to new opportunities, many government bureaus still work according to cumbersome old school rules. Without a contact you will never get beyond the reception desk.

# 9    Strategies for Success

Argentines aren't ones for strict schedules. In fact, canceling without prior warning, while less common than in years past, still occurs. As a result, non-Argentines who are on a sales trip should patiently roll with the punches. Avoid scheduling appointments too close together and prepare to make several trips to the country before a deal is closed. Visitors in a buying or investing mode will find the Argentines more punctual.

Argentines will often criticize shortcomings or inefficiencies in their system that a foreigner might also observe. However, even when they are criticizing their own nation, it's best not to join in on the critique. Argentina may stand in need of modern technology and fresh capital, but they won't do business with someone who rubs them the wrong way. Argentines not only have faith in their own capabilities, but they can be choosey when it comes to letting foreigners have the "privilege" of investing or working in Argentina.

## 10 Golden Rules

1. **Learn about the Country**

One would be making a mistake to group Argentina with the rest of South America. Don't try to establish a rapport with your potential colleague by referring to previous experiences in other Latin American countries. It may be misconstrued as stereotyping. While some Westerners may see some general similarities, Argentines generally don't. They consider your having some specific knowledge about their country to be a compliment. Knowing a bit about Argentina's past will also help you to understand your counterpart's background and what the culture considers important.

Identify publications and organizations pertinent to your endeavor and obtain as much information as possible. Talk to business colleagues or organizations who have had dealings with Argentina to gain some insights into this quixotic, often contradictory, and rapidly changing country. Make extensive use of the Internet to research and network with emerging market specialists.

2. **Make Local Contacts**

Spread your net of potential contacts as wide as possible. But while you will need to call to make an initial contact and discover who the person is you should be dealing with, following up with letters and faxes will help to cement your presence in their minds. Keep in mind that contacts from urban areas may be of little use in the countryside and vice versa. Avoid setting up a meeting months before you arrive, however. At the very most, attempt to coordinate a meeting several weeks before you plan to visit Argentina, otherwise you may likely find it canceled.

3.  **Pick the Right Partner**

As gifted speakers, Argentines might promise you the moon if you asked. Thus, make sure that you and your Argentine colleague share the same values and expectations, particularly in regards to detail, quality, quantity, and follow-through. If possible, visit your potential partner's offices or factory to acquire some on-site knowledge of how things work. Also consider it a good idea to ask around the industry to get an idea about what other Argentines think about a potential colleague's work. Even better, check with the local expatriate community to see how your potential partner stands with them.

4.  **Put it in Writing . . . Diplomatically**

*Las palabras se le lleva el viento*—words are blown away with the wind—is an Argentine saying. Hence, put any agreements in writing—even those reached before the final contract is signed.

Also, Argentines can come across as frank and direct, but they also take pride in exhibiting tact and diplomacy. In both speech and writing they can appear indirect, elaborate, and almost poetic in the way they express themselves. As such, instead of writing letters or faxes that an Argentine may perceive as cold and dry, try to lace your prose with polite and thoughtful compliments.

5.  **Avoid casting blame**

Argentines don't take well to direct confrontation or blame. Either mention the problem indirectly as something that needs attention, or ignore it.

6.  **Time**

Anyone working in Argentina must view time as a flexible commodity. Nothing can be rushed. Prepare to make several trips and to schedule meetings at any time of the day or night. Schedules are very much a function of who is buying or selling.

### 7.   Learn the Language

Many Argentines, especially those working at the executive level, speak English as the language of global commerce. However, they consider your efforts to learn Argentine Spanish as a sign of goodwill. Spanish may also prove essential for working in the provinces or dealing with lower-level employees. You might also find that the president of the company and the secretary speak English or another European language, but that the manager of the department with whom you will deal only speaks Spanish.

Although you can communicate without it, to get the gist of a lot of Argentine conversation, consider it a good idea to learn a few words of slang Lunfardo. Argentine book stores carry Lunfardo dictionaries, or look for them on the Internet.

### 8.   Looks Count

Although it is important to be trustworthy and well-connected, your appearance remains primary to setting a good first impression. Elegance and sophistication are tantamount. One should dress impeccably, stand straight, and look your host in the eye.

### 9.   *Vos* vs. *Usted*

It's safest to start by greeting someone you don't know with the formal *usted* when using Spanish. Older people commonly use, or are referred to by *usted*; but younger generations almost immediately lapse into the more familiar *vos*.

### 10.  Be Tactful

Argentines can appear argumentative and hold some very strong opinions. At the same time, they take pride in being polite and diplomatic. Always defer to the side of tactfulness and carefully worded speech to get your point of across. While bursts of emotion and raised voices are common among Argentines, foreigners will do best to keep their cool.

# 10   Time

Time is not something to be hurried or rigidly compartmentalized in Argentina. Rather, it is to be enjoyed. Tomorrow brings another day and, as a result, things will take longer than foreigners expect.

## Punctuality

Although Argentines expect you to arrive promptly, meetings rarely begin on time. Meetings scheduled before 10 A.M. usually become an exercise in waiting, so try and push the meeting up to a later slot, if possible. Always confirm a meeting time a few hours before arriving as businesspeople often cancel meetings or reschedule without notice. Upon arriving you may be asked to wait and don't be surprised if, after waiting, your contact hurries you out because of another appointment. While some apologize profusely for keeping you waiting, some may make no excuse at all.

## Interruptions

Once in the meeting, you will likely experience several interruptions. Along with the requisite coffee or mate service, secretaries will walk in with messages and your Argentine partner will accept several phone calls—anyone from his children to his business partners; he may even ask a colleague to sit in on the meeting. Argentines don't usually exhibit any qualms about dealing with personal matters in the middle of a meeting either—from dictating instructions to the interior decorator, to ironing out vacation plans with the travel agent. Much of this is an attempt to demonstrate who is controlling the situation.

Lunch dates begin on time, but guests should arrive 20 to 30 minutes late for business dinners or cocktails. If you have any doubts about what time to arrive, ask if you should set your watch by *hora americana* (American time) or *hora argentina* (Argentine time).

## Flexible Deadlines

Despite well-intentioned assurances to the contrary, deadlines will come and deadlines will go as it serves the Argentine partner. Continue checking up on people. Make it clear that you expect the deadline to be met, and even then, it requires further follow up.

Your Argentine counterpart may very well be interested in closing a deal, but he will often calculate a deadline without realistically gauging his own capabilities. He may get distracted with other commitments or become enthused over a new project. Encourage him to stay focused on his commitment to you.

# 11   Business Meetings

### Phone Phobia vs. Cellphone Mania

While North Americans rely heavily on telephones to conduct business, Argentines prefer to meet face-to-face. Phone service in Argentina has improved markedly from just a few years ago when it was difficult to get a line, and even if obtained it would often suffer spontaneous disconnection. Still, an anonymous voice on the other end of the line doesn't fit well with Argentines' personalized style of doing business. Argentines feel the need to assess your character, taste in clothes, and dependability, which proves difficult over the phone. Generally speaking, Argentines only use the phone to set up an initial interview. Once a relationship has been established, however, they find that doing business over the phone can provide convenience and more efficiency.

Despite a general mistrust of phones, Argentines are massive cellular phone users—Buenos Aires boasts the highest concentration of mobile phone users in Latin America. Mobile phones appeal not only to the Argentines' love for electronic gadgets but for social relations. A cell phone is a necessary accessory for almost all businesspeople—as well as for their spouses and children. Even the many dog walkers in Buenos Aires, who often walk up to 30 dogs at a time, have discovered cellular phones are an essential tool for doing business. For those without a cell phone, they can turn to taxis that rent phones to passengers.

## Laying Good Groundwork

In making your initial contacts with an Argentine company, it's still a good idea to start with a phone call. This will ensure that the person whom you have been advised to contact is actually the best individual with whom to speak. Since Argentines rarely, if ever, return phone messages or correspondence, you may discover too late that you have wasted valuable time trying to establish a dialogue with the wrong person.

Once you know whom your best contact will be, write a letter or send a fax. Try to sound diplomatic and include some background information about yourself. Try to set up an interview one to two weeks in advance of your arrival as Argentines rarely schedule any farther in advance. An Argentine executive tells the story of how exasperated she was by a foreign media group which called her regularly for six months to confirm a meeting in Buenos Aires. "How am I supposed to know what I'll be doing then? Who can plan that far ahead? Maybe I won't feel like going to a meeting that day."

## The First Meeting

Don't be surprised if an Argentine cancels a first meeting. Until a relationship is established, your Argentine colleague will feel free to call off a meeting if more important business arises subject to the buyer/seller relationship. When the appointment is held, expect a warm welcome. Argentines genuinely show interest in meeting new people — particularly foreigners in a buying mode.

Avoid launching directly into your business proposal. Prepare to make small talk at the beginning of the meeting, perhaps over a cup of coffee. If your host knows anything about your country, he will want to discuss his impressions with you as well as your thoughts on Argentina. He will prefer to settle down and get comfortable with you in order to assess whether, as people, you can do business together. Never exhibit urgency or impatience to get down to business. Argentines consider impatience one of the main cultural "failings" of non-Latinos.

## Mastering Subtlety

When your colleague is ready to discuss business, he will refer to it indirectly. To prove that you are "serious" about working with him, it's a good idea to be well versed in his company's background as well as that of the sector. Since the fate of most industry in Argentina remains closely tied to the country's political and economic ups and downs, prepare yourself with some basic knowledge of Argentine history.

Your ability to speak Spanish becomes advantageous in establishing a stronger bond. Argentines like to show that they speak other languages, however, and will often offer to speak a few phrases of your language with you. As a sign of goodwill, some introductory comments by you in Spanish will be appreciated.

## Name-Dropping

Since your contacts in Argentina may prove to be your most important resource, name-dropping is one way to an Argentine's heart—but only to a certain extent. Knowing too many people will raise alarm bells with Argentines wary of the well-known *piolo argentino*. At the same time, take care not to one-up your Argentine host, remembering his sensitivity to social status and negative reaction to what he might construe as attitudes of superiority.

Most of the prebusiness conversation will revolve around politics, history, and your personal situation. Argentines express keen curiosity about whether you are married or not, how long you've been married, and if you have children. Remember that family life is very important in Argentine culture and don't take offense.

## Too Good to be True

Your Argentine colleague may appear very enthusiastic, which could either mean he's interested or just being polite. Don't be surprised if he invites you for lunch or even an *asado* at his *quinta*, or country home. He may also genuinely want to follow up with another meeting—but it is your duty to make sure it happens.

The initial meeting may run even longer than you expected. Still, when the time has come to make an exit, don't rush out. An Argentine may view such a quick departure as rude or unreliable behavior. Always end the appointment with a few more minutes of small talk before leaving. If your Argentine colleague appears interested, ask him if you can call on him again. If he replies positively, ask him for a convenient time.

# 12 Negotiating with Argentines

Argentines have honed their people skills to a fine art. Before they even sit down at a negotiating table, they have assessed your character and learned your thoughts on family, culture, politics, and the economy. Adept and persuasive, they will appeal to personal relations to obtain concessions. If that doesn't work, they may resort to temperamental outbursts. Don't reciprocate.

## Under Pressure

While Argentines will feel free to pressure you, responding in kind may backfire on you as a foreign negotiator. If they perceive that you have exploited an Argentine weakness or that you have taken undue advantage of them, they are liable to walk away from a deal. If you do get them to sign on under duress, they may not fulfill their contractual obligations.

Instead, prepare a list of positions the other side might take and develop alternatives. Try to put yourself in Argentine shoes and make an effort to separate personalities from economic issues. While such efforts are time-consuming and extremely involved, try to remain patient. If you exhibit urgency or impatience, you may not only offend your Argentine counterparts, but they may in turn exploit it as a weakness. Goodwill goes a long way, and while you need to be shrewd, you must absolutely ensure that your Argentine colleagues believe that you play the game fairly.

## Tips for Foreign Negotiators

1. **Know with whom you are dealing.**

   Acquire a thorough knowledge of the company with which you intend to do business. Review the details of the project, its goals, and the personnel involved. To get a feel for how the company operates, interview businesspeople who have dealt with the company in the past and study any contracts the company may have had with other firms. Note that Argentinian firms have gained notoriety for inaccurately reporting their costs and revenues.

2. **Use independent references.**

   Dependable statistical information is hard to come by in Argentina. People often quote numbers off the top of the head, which usually prove inaccurate. Try your best to find reliable, objective measures on which to base your proposal. A government statistics bureau provides information, as do private market studies. Expatriates are another source. If you have taken these preliminary steps, your Argentine counterpart will find it difficult to sway you based on emotion or your lack of familiarity with the market.

3. **Don't play all your cards at once.**

   Argentines are skilled negotiators. To make the most of a deal, play your cards one at a time—but do it tactfully and amiably. Argentines don't appreciate abrasiveness or confrontation. They regard a take-it-or-leave-it approach as insulting, a challenge rather than part of the game.

**4.  Take it seriously.**

One of the first complaints that an Argentine will make about a foreign colleague is that he's "not serious." To show that you mean business, listen carefully and take lots of notes. Repeat key points to avoid confusion and to show that you regard their business as important. Prepare to sit quietly for long stretches of time as well; it gives the appearance of deliberate consideration and may result in additional concessions from the other side. When buying or investing, remain impassive and let the Argentine side play themselves out. Use every occasion possible to assure the Argentine team that you are thinking long-term and thereby interested in satisfying mutual concerns.

**5.  Be prepared to walk away.**

If you don't feel comfortable with the terms of a deal, it's best to walk away—but do it tactfully. Placing blame or departing in a huff is liable to backfire. Since Argentine business is highly personalized, an insult will leave a bad impression and word will get around so that you may find other business avenues or future deals closed to your interests.

## Argentine Negotiating Strategies

The Argentines see themselves as very sophisticated and worldly negotiators. Justifiably or not, they believe they have few rivals when it comes to negotiating savvy. A consequence of this attitude is that they have a highly developed strategy for every negotiating situation.

When involved in trade talks the Argentines tend toward one of the following strategies:

**Impassive** – They permit you to lay out your

entire trade package without comment. They then "cherry-pick" those portions they find most favorable while rejecting the rest.

**Aggressive** – Argentines in a buying mode will run roughshod over your proposal and demand that you concede every point in their favor. This is a very macho maneuver and difficult to overcome if you are not prepared.

**Stubborn** – When in a selling mode, Argentines will remain steadfast and repeat their proposal in various forms with no real changes to the content. The repetitive nature of the strategy works well on an opposition with a tight schedule.

**Social** – Very commonly used when looking for buyers or investors, an Argentine negotiator will turn on the charm. Cocktail parties, theater tickets, invitations to family events will all be used to lull you into a sense of friendship that will be exploited at the negotiating table.

**Hierarchical** – This is the very nature of most Argentine businesses and they use the structure to run foreign sellers through a confusing chain of command. The object is to wear down an opponent before getting to the final contract.

## The Argentine Approach to Contracts

A handshake and a verbal agreement don't go very far in Argentina. An agreement can change significantly before a final contract is signed. Seasoned negotiators will recommend signing a written understanding at each stage of an agreement until you reach a complete contract.

But while contracts were once simple and straightforward, they have becoming increasingly complex with the influx of foreign investment brought in under the privatization program. Argentines welcome the added security of more binding, all-encompassing, detail-oriented legal agreements made standard by U.S. corporations. They will also make sure to carefully scrutinize all contracts through legal and financial professionals, thus foreign businesspeople should do the same. Leave nothing open to interpretation.

If you come from a society where contracts are sealed with a "handshake," Argentina will break you of the habit. Bear in mind that contracts are only enforceable in the local language. Do not accept the translated copy for signature until the original has been independently interpreted.

## 13 Business Outside the Law

### The Underground Economy

According to a well known Argentine saying, *el que no afana es un gil*—he that doesn't rip you off is stupid. That saying is borne out in a variety of ways, beginning with tax evasion. Considered a national pastime, it is estimated that Argentines actually pay only 60 percent of taxes owed. After a parallel customs ring was discovered in 1996, believed to have bilked the government of $3 billion in customs revenue, the government decided to crack down on tax dodgers. It merged customs and the internal revenue service to create a "super" ministry. Their efforts have included everything from surprise raids to enacting criminal offense procedures if a merchant fails to give a receipt upon request. (The government even awarded a woman 1 million pesos for sending in her sales receipts to help build a government case.)

Still, if anyone wishes to buy stolen merchandise or cheap copies of expensive brand names, they need only cross the border to the frontier town of Cuidad del Este in Paraguay. A kind of no-man's land, the city has not only gained fame as a known terrorist refuge, but also as the continental capital of stolen cars, contraband, and cheap Asian imports.

Intellectual property rights also remain a problem in Argentina. The U.S. Department of Commerce has placed the country on its priority watch list for poor patent protection. After heavy U.S. pressure, Argentina passed a law in 1996 to protect industrial secrets, particularly as they relate to pharmaceutical patents. Industry groups who say they lose $540 million a year in pirated patents maintain, however, that the law is ineffective. Argentina also lacks copyright protection for software and high-tech companies estimate about 70 percent of all programs (even software programs found in government institutions) are pirated.

## Graft and Corruption

According to the European consultancy, Transparency International, Argentina ranks 25th out of the 81 countries ranked in terms of corruption. Reports surface almost daily in the press of scandals involving government officials all the way up to President Menem and the president's brother-in-law.

According to Menem and many businesspeople, however, corruption has diminished significantly since state-owned enterprises, considered focal points of corruption, were sold off to private interests. Still, corruption has become a rallying cry for opposition political parties, and opinion polls show the population considers it a top concern after unemployment. The feelings of indignation are exacerbated by a heavily manipulated justice system. Of the hundreds of government functionaries accused of crimes, none have ever gone to jail while dozens, including several judges, remain fugitives of justice.

It should be noted that Argentina has no more and no less corruption than most of the world's emerging markets. All businesspeople preparing to travel to Argentina should determine in advance how they will deal with any corrupt practices they might encounter. Be aware that there is a growing movement to punish businesspeople in their home market for offenses committed abroad.

## Sex and Prostitution

Recent changes to the legal code of Buenos Aires have made prostitution legal. Prostitutes in the city already have their own union as well as hotels specially dedicated to the trade. An abundance of *albergues transitorios*—transitory hostels—exist. In the downtown core, runners distribute pamphlets listing hourly prices, and there is talk of establishing an official red-light district. Nonetheless, it remains a cause of social conflict in this very Catholic country with strong family traditions.

# Names & Greetings

First impressions count in Argentina. Thus, one should be aware that an Argentine begins by physically sizing up a foreigner. When you meet someone, try to strike a balance between self-confidence and discretion, professionalism and amiability. Argentines recognize that a foreigner may not be used to being greeted with a kiss on the cheek and will offer to shake your hand. But once you've made the rounds they will welcome you into the fold with a kiss—although it may happen more quickly with women than with men.

## Vos vs. Usted

Foreigners always wonder whether to use *vos* or *usted* when addressing colleagues. To start, use the more formal and respectful *usted*. Among older people, lower echelon workers such as maids and doormen, and in more traditionally run family businesses *usted* is commonly used. In most cases, the change over to *vos* occurs almost immediately. Your host may ask if he can *tutear* you, or refer to you in the familiar second person. Just follow his lead.

Argentina remains the only country other than

Uruguay to use *vos* in the Spanish second person. So, if you are used to speaking more traditional Spanish, which uses *tu* in the second person, feel comfortable continuing to do so. Argentines will understand and will sometimes switch to *tu* to make it easier for you.

## Order and Gender

Argentine businesspeople usually write their first names followed by their family name. A tradition in many Spanish speaking countries, they may or may not have a second last name. Women often attach their married name to their maiden name with *de*. Many Argentines have a double first name such as Juan José or María Angelica.

Because of immigration and heavy influence from Europe, and increasingly from North America, Argentines will sometimes take on English names such as Janice or Kevin but pronounce it with a Spanish accent. As a sign of friendship they will shorten names, changing Andrea to Andre or Rodrigo to Rodri. Like most Latinos, they are also very fond of diminutives such as Evita for Eva or Manuelito instead of Manuel. Argentines also refer to each other using short physical descriptions such as *linda* (pretty); although most may sound more derogatory, they are actually terms of affection. Some of the more common names include *gordo* (fatso), *flaco* (skinny), or *viejo* (old man).

Address married women as *señora* and young, unmarried women as *señorita,* followed by the surname, e.g., Señora Vazquez or Señorita Andreani.

## A Nation of Titles

Argentines widely use academic and professional titles. "It's nobility made in Argentina," says one businessman, and it's an insult not to use them. Make a point of learning whether your colleague uses a title before a meeting. *Licenciado*, written *Lic.*, presides as the most common title and refers to someone with a university degree. Refer to engineers as *Ingeniero* or *Ing.* in writing, while an architect is called *Architecto*, which is shortened to *Arch.* *Doctor* (or *Doctora* for a woman) is commonly used for lawyers, economists, researchers, and other professionals with Ph.D. level degrees.

## Un Beso

Until about ten years ago, a handshake served as the standard greeting between male colleagues. It has since been replaced by a kiss on the cheek. "It's suddenly become fashionable for men to kiss," says a 40-year-old executive. For close friends and partners, a generous handshake, hug, and a pat on the back usually accompanies the kiss. Argentines greet first-time foreign male acquaintances with just a handshake although women, whether they know each other or not, kiss. Instead of saying *chao* or good-bye when they get off the phone, Argentines say *un beso* (a kiss) or *un abrazo* (a hug).

## The Business Card Exchange

Unlike other countries such as Japan, Argentines do not place great worth on exchanging business cards. Some Argentines may give you their business card immediately after meeting while others may carry none. Try to get a business card since it usually includes their direct line or *interno* (extension number), which will allow you to avoid the oftentimes consuming process of going through a central number or several receptionists.

 **Communication Styles**

### Conversation Starters

Argentines are usually quite open to meeting new people. To establish a personal bond, which is advised in any business relationship, it is polite to ask about your colleague's family, including their marital status and if they have children. They will ask the same questions of you, although you may do best to let them initiate the conversation. Argentines are curious about the personal background of any newcomer as well as their impressions of Argentina and why he has chosen to do business in the country. They are impressed with foreigners who have taken an interest in the local culture and history. It could range from thoughts about their most famous writer, Jorge Luis Borges, to the rivalry between Buenos Aires' two leading soccer teams, Boca Juniors and River Plate. Popular subjects with Argentines also include movies, music, and food.

### Conversation Landmines

Certain topics may make your Argentine host or potential business partner uncomfortable.

**Politics.** Avoid politics unless your Argentine counterpart brings it up first. Nonetheless, the subject will almost inevitably come up since most Argentines, from the doorman to the company C.E.O., take a personal interest in the country's politics. They might ask you what you think of President Carlos Menem's administration or the legacy of General Perón and his wife Eva. In any case, your local colleague's personal opinion will not likely be middle-of-the-road. Visitors from the United States, Germany, and the United Kingdom will be of particular interest to the Argentines but for very different reasons.

**The 1976-1983 Dictatorship.** The *guerra sucia,* or Dirty War as it is also known, is still a deeply divisive issue in Argentine society considering an estimated 9,000 to 30,000 people are *desaparecidos* (missing). Among the upper echelons of society and intellectual groups, it's very likely a family member was kidnapped by leftist guerrillas or killed by the military; as such, you will do best not to mention the dictatorship.

**The Falkland/Malvinas Islands War.** Argentines are taught from childhood to believe the islands, under British control, belong to Argentina. The 1982 war to return the islands to Argentine sovereignty served as a humiliating defeat for the Argentine military and remains an emotional topic. Always remember to refer to the islands by their Argentine name, *Islas Malvinas.*

**Relations with Chile.** While a safer topic than in previous years, Argentines still retain much resentment toward Chileans over historic border disputes, which they interpret as a gratuitous land grab. Chile has even had the temerity to outpace Argentina in GDP per capita. In fact, due to regional rivalries and wars, praising any of Argentina's neighbors proves iffy.

**Racism.** Argentines will insist they aren't racist. Nevertheless, you are likely to hear racially related remarks or jokes considered "politically incorrect" in North America or Europe. To avoid a heated debate, it's best to ignore.

**Boasting.** While it's helpful for your colleagues to know you are professionally accomplished, discretion is advised. Boasting leads to distrust.

**Age and Money.** Argentines will readily ask you your age but consider it crass to talk about how much money you earn.

## Nonverbal Communication

Due to an Argentine's affectionate nature, personal space is reduced from what some Westerners and Asians are used to. In conversation don't be surprised if you are repeatedly touched on the arm—a pat on the shoulder is a sign of friendship. When standing in line, prepare for crowding and bumping. Stand your ground or prepare to lose your turn.

## Guidelines

Since Argentines show intense interest in how you differ from them (and will make you aware of it as well), try to meld in by mimicking their communication style.

**Be Physical.** Argentines are very *cariñosa* or affectionate. Along with shaking hands, Argentines usually kiss each other on the cheek in greeting and, if they are good friends, will also exchange a pat on the back or a hug.

**Stand Close.** Argentines are truly "in your face" during a conversation. Restrain yourself from trying to back away since an Argentine will probably step closer to close the distance. Argentines only allow a wide berth when privacy seems to be a requisite such as waiting to use a bank machine. (As a rule of thumb, wait outside the glass cubicle while someone else withdraws money.)

**Speak Softly.** Compared to some Western and Asian countries, the sound level of conversation in bars or restaurants is much higher. Nonetheless, speaking loudly is considered crude in private conversation.

**Don't Point.** Argentines consider pointing with your finger to be rude. To indicate something, use your entire hand with an open palm.

**Posture Counts.** Argentines often think of North Americans and some Europeans as looking too stiff. Standing straight, however, and keeping your hands out of your pockets are marks of good manners.

**Maintain Eye Contact.** When talking to someone, look them in the eye. Avoiding eye contact will make you appear untrustworthy. Visitors from Asia, where such action is disrespectful among strangers, may find this behavior disconcerting.

**Ask Permission.** Whether getting up from the table, trying to get around someone in the street, or making your way to your seat in a movie, always say *permiso*, the English equivalent of "excuse me."

# 16 Customs

### Cafes – The Center of Social Life

The smoke-filled interiors, mirrored walls, and rich, wooden moldings of Argentina's many cafes have acted as the setting for numerous angst-ridden Tangos, such as *El Ultimo Cafe* (The Last Cafe). They are also the preferred work environment for some of the country's greatest writers. The center of Argentina's social life, cafes offer a meeting ground for everyone from liberal intellectuals, to politicians, businesspeople, journalists, and taxi drivers to discuss business and the state of the world.

Buenos Aires boasts several classic turn-of-the-century cafes or *confiterias* such as the Cafe Tortoni, a popular tourist stop. Dating from 1853, the venerable cafe and Porteño institution features Belle Époque chandeliers, marble columns, Tango and jazz shows, and is home to the Lunfardo Association.

The standard fare at most cafes includes snacks or *picadas* of cheese, cold cuts, olives, nuts or chips, and lightweight or quick meals. Toasted white bread sandwiches with ham and cheese are known as *tostados*. Cafes also serve pizza, along with *lomito* (steak sandwich), *panchos* (hot dogs), and *milanesas*, which are schnitzels. Coffee, which is quite good, is served espresso style, but comes in several varieties as well as sizes.

## Mate

Also known as Paraguayan tea after its origins, this bitter green herb provides Argentina with its greatest pleasure and most important social ritual. "Mate is my relaxation," says a domestic worker. "When I'm drinking mate I can't do anything else." Argentina is the world's largest producer and consumer of mate. Its population consumes an average 5 kilograms of the leaves per person a year, more than four times the average intake of coffee.

Both its preparation and its consumption follow strict social norms that transcend class and ethnicity. A hollowed-out gourd is packed two-thirds full with the chopped, dried *yerba mate* leaf. Warm, but not boiled, water is poured to the top of the gourd, producing a slight froth. The liquid is drunk through a steel straw, known as a *bombilla*, which sports a perforated bulbous tip. The first few sips are spit out. Often shared among a group, one person is charged with emptying out the gourd before it is refilled and passed on to the next person.

One can often observe Argentines carrying a thermos full of hot water for mate and it's not uncommon to find government officials nursing *mates* in their offices. A refreshing stimulant, mate packs more caffeine then coffee, gets rid of hunger pains, and also serves as a remedy for mild intestinal and stomach upsets. The holders, also called mates, vary greatly from plain squash gourds, hollowed-out cow horns, to elaborate silver holders often seen in museums.

## El Picnic

When arriving at Argentina's international airport outside Buenos Aires, the visitor will be struck by the number of families picnicking and playing soccer by the side of the multilane highway. Despite Argentina's abundant land, publicly accessible green space remains scarce due to the high value placed on private property. As a result, one will find the busiest parts of Buenos Aires as the chosen spot for sunbathers and picnickers—who come completely prepared with tables, chairs, the family dog, and of course, mate.

## Country Life

For those who can afford to get away from the urban hustle and bustle, there are a multitude of *quintas* or *barrios privados*, which have recently sprung up on the outskirts of the cities. Country-style homes located in walled communities have become popular among the upper middle class, who desert Buenos Aires in droves on the weekends to horseback ride, play soccer, and relax by their swimming pools.

## Land of Shrines

Argentina's highways are littered with shrines by the side of the road. But not all of them pay homage to the thousands of Argentines who die every year in accidents caused by the country's chaotic traffic. Many of the miniature chapels are filled with offerings of water to the *Difunta Correa*, a woman who died of thirst in the deserts of San Juan province during the wars of independence yet whose corpse miraculously continued to nurse her baby. In San Juan, an impressive shrine was resur-

rected to remember the miracle, and every year
thousands visit to ask the Difunta Correa for divine
guidance.

## Regional Music and Dance

Tango's heart-rending lyrics, mournful music,
and defiant dance steps reflect a nostalgic, often
melancholy Buenos Aires. In the provinces, the rich
musical heritage becomes steeped in folklore and
the country's more earthy roots. Many of the
dances and their music, such as the *Gato, Chacarera,*
and *Escondida,* which are accompanied by a guitar
and a drum, follow the cadence of a cantering
horse. In the *Malambo,* the gaucho shows off his
fancy footwork with the help of spurs and handkerchiefs. The *Zamba* also uses a kerchief, but is danced
between couples and moves in a slower and more
stately manner.

In the province of Buenos Aires, gauchos sing
*Milongas, Estilos,* and *Cifras.* In the Puna, or the high
plains near the Bolivian border, *Bailecitos* and
*Carnevalitos* dances are accompanied by the high-
pitched music of the *Vidalitas* and *Bagualas.* The
northeastern provinces of Corrientes and Missiones
dance the *Polca* and *Galopa* accompanied by the
accordion and harp sounds of the *Chamamé.*

# 17  Dress & Appearance

Argentines make a point to keep up with the latest styles abroad. They will often fly to Europe to purchase the upcoming season's fashions before they debut on the streets of Milan or London. Argentines have a pronounced Italian accent to their clothing style and even when they dress casually, they manage to look sophisticated.

Businessmen tend to wear dark suits, silk socks, handkerchiefs, and are often avid tie collectors. They consider cuff links particularly elegant and commonly wear ascots. Compared to their North American counterparts, businesswomen might wear more revealing clothes and appear perfectly coiffed at all times. Beauty salons stay open late Friday and Saturday nights to see their female customers off to cocktail parties, the theater, or just dinner with friends and family.

City wear and country clothes remain markedly different, however. While most Argentines dress up to go downtown, when visiting *estancias* or *quintas* in the country they tend to don more rustic, albeit tasteful, attire. Gaucho-style clothes have also begun to make a comeback. One will commonly see Argentines, particularly in the country, wearing *pantalones bombachas,* loose-fitting pants that tie at the bottom, and *alpargatas* (flat cloth shoes) or leather boots. It is not advisable, however, to wear native Indian clothes. Persons attending an asado usually wear casual but slightly dressy resort clothes.

While shoppers procure their more fashionable clothes in Europe or Miami, Argentina is the place for leather goods. Although one must carefully inspect workmanship, leather coats, shoes, wallets, belts, vests, and luggage are in abundance. Along with cow leather, a softer suede made from the hide of *carpincho* or capybara (the world's largest rodent) is also widely available. The more well-known leather houses include Maggio & Rossetto and Rossi y Caruso.

Summers are hot and humid, so bring summer clothes made of lightweight material. At the slightest hint of cold weather, Porteños will bring out the camel hair coats for men and furs for women; but for those used to harsher climates, a wool suit and overcoat will do. Whatever you wear in whichever season, make sure it is in good repair, clean, and well-pressed.

 **Reading the Argentines**

### Style vs. Substance

In keeping with their Italian inclinations, Argentines rely heavily on body language to communicate. Facial expressions and physical gestures go far to achieve a unique dramatic effect. An Argentine's body language often expresses his mood or affection (or lack thereof) toward someone or something. "With gestures you don't need to say anything," notes one Argentine. If you want to be subtle, you speak.

- Whistling or hissing through one's teeth to get someone's attention is common.

- Argentines cover their mouth when yawning, coughing, or using a toothpick.

- Cupping one's hand and touching the thumb to the fingers in a point and then moving the hand back and forth is a sarcastic way of saying "What is this?" or "What do you want?" Passing one's fingers under the chin, palm open, while pointing the corners of one's mouth down and raising one's eyebrows means, "What do I care?" or "I don't get it."

- The classic okay sign in the United States — thumb and forefinger forming a circle and other fingers pointing up—means the same thing in Argentina.

- Eye contact is a statement of assurance and confidence. Therefore, consider direct eye contact on the street or in a restaurant too personal; someone may view such an action as a pickup. Refusing to meet someone's eye during a business meeting indicates you may not be trustworthy.

- Counting on one's fingers begins with the pinkie finger and moves along the hand until reaching the thumb.

- Spitting, while common, is considered rude. Pointing is also impolite.

- The Gaelic shoulder shrug alone means "I don't care." A hand raised to the cheek, palm open, with shoulders up, means "I don't know."

- To beckon you, an Argentine will extend his arm, palm down, and make a scratching motion with his fingers.

- Avoid placing your hands on your hips (arms akimbo) since an Argentine will take it as a sign of anger or a challenge.

- Eating in the street or on public transportation is considered impolite.

## Entertaining

### Pure Carnivores

Beef, to Argentines, is as sacred as Tango and Eva Perón. Whether skewered over an open pit in the countryside or served up in restaurants featuring cow-hide motifs in the capital of Buenos Aires, Argentines eat, in almost ritualistic fashion, an impressive 123 pounds of beef per capita a year. Believe it or not, the number of pounds consumed has significantly lessened from just a decade ago.

Argentines do not find it uncommon to eat a steak for lunch, although the cuts are different and much larger than to what most Westerners are accustomed. Because of the sheer importance of meat, a visitor will do well to have some familiarity with the basic cuts before dining with an Argentine host. The most popular choices include: *colita de cuadril* (rump roast), *vacio* (porterhouse and flank), *bife de chorizo* (sirloin), *bife de lomo* (short tenderloin), and *bife de costilla* (T-bone). You can order your beef *jugoso* (medium rare), *a punto* (medium), while well done is *cocido*. To Argentines meat or *carne* only refers to beef. Other types of meat, including lamb, pork, and chicken, are referred to by their respective names.

The asado, or barbecue, represents the classic meat-eating experience in Argentina. People will often hold an asado in someone's home or in special restaurants called *parilladas*. A variety of meats and entrails are served up at an asado, the quantity of which most non-Argentines don't normally eat in the space of a week or even a month. Some specialties include *chinchulines* (small intestine), *ubre* (udder), *mollejas* (sweetbreads), *morcilla* (blood sausage), and *matambre*, which is flank steak served hot or in a cold roll. While Argentines usually avoid condiments or spices on their food other than salt, *chimichurri*—a marinade made from garlic, parsley, ground peppers, oil, and vinegar—can accompany an asado.

## Wine

Argentina ranks as the fourth largest wine producer in the world. Until recently, it's prodigious wine-making capabilities were a well-kept secret since Argentines managed to drink the country's entire national production. Argentines drink an average of 44 liters of wine per person a year, placing them just behind France, Italy, Spain, and Luxembourg in world per capita consumption. They used to drink nearly double that amount, but beer and soft drinks have slowly replaced wine as more popular beverages. Due to previous economic instability, the country's harvested area has been cut by a third since the 1960s. Only with the introduction of market-oriented reforms in the early 1990s did the industry begin to blossom once again.

Since then, Argentine wineries (1,500 in total) have followed in the footsteps of California and Australia, investing some US$150 million to make bolder tasting wine and bottling it in sleek new packaging. Thus far, efforts have proven fruitful. As the latest edition to the group of "New World" wines rising to challenge the industry icons of Europe, Argentine sales of fine wines abroad jumped 300 percent between 1994 and 1997. The emphasis on fine wine production over that of bulk wines has won Argentina international accolades, particularly for its Malbec wines, which have found ideal climatic conditions in the semidesert province of Mendoza. Other wine-producing provinces include San Juan, La Rioja, and Salta, from which the unique, sweet white wine *Torrontés* originates.

The Jesuits first introduced wine to Argentina in the 17th century for use in communion at church services. The real boom in production came with the heavy immigration of Italian, French, and Spanish, who brought grape varieties with them from Europe. The most popular varieties include cabernet sauvignon, chardonnay, merlot, and chenin blanc. Argentina's pioneer vintners didn't pay much attention to the various wine categories, however. The liberal use of wine denominations from other countries has now prompted Argentina to reorganize its industry by international guidelines to avert a potential commercial backlash.

## Other Spirits

Big fans of sparkling wine, commonly referred to as *champan* (champagne), Argentines often serve it at parties, weddings, and as a drink before dinner. Other popular drinks include *sidra*, a sweet alcoholic drink made from apples, and *clerico*, sparkling wine mixed with fruit and served like sangria in a large jug.

## Crazy for Dulce de Leche

To satisfy Argentines' tremendous sweet tooth, *confiterias* and *panaderias* (bakeries) offer an impressive variety of cakes, cookies, and *facturas*, which literally means bill but in Argentina means pastries. Eaten in the morning as well as the late afternoon as a snack, each factura has its own name, including *media lunas* (a variation on the French croissant), *pan de leche, vigilantes,* and *chorros,* a sugary dough in the shape of a Doric column. But despite the variety, all desserts usually have one of two basic ingredients: meringue, made with egg white or *dulce de leche,* a kind of caramelized milk that comes in a startling number of shapes and forms. It can be served either on top of flan, as an ice cream flavor, as icing on or filling in pastries, or right out of the bottle like peanut butter. It is also a particular favorite among pregnant women.

As in Italy, ice cream in Argentina has been raised to an art form. Often *elaboracion artesanal,* or homemade, Argentines eat ice cream year-round, any time of day.

## Restaurant Dining

One may almost consider dining out as a social mandate in Argentina, and lunch proves a popular venue for getting to know potential business partners. Lasting at least two hours, the noon meal usually begins with a glass of *champan* and rarely ends without a *cortado,* an espresso coffee with a little milk, and dessert. In between, prepare for copious amounts of meat. Vegetables aren't included with any plate of beef and must be ordered on the side. Business lunches are less common in the provinces, where many people still go home for the mid-day meal.

An Argentine may or may not discuss actual business during a meal. As such, one should consider lunch as an important way of establishing a network of contacts and developing personal relations. One should revisit any previously discussed points of business during a lunch meeting that takes place in an office setting.

Prodigious smokers, Argentines will most likely smoke throughout the meal. If you smoke, make a point of offering. Some Argentines may ask if you mind their smoking in your presence, but they expect a negative answer. Otherwise, European-style table manners are the norm.

Argentines do not normally share the bill. He who invites should pay. Thus, consider it a polite gesture to avoid ordering imported liquors since hefty taxes make them very costly. Try one of the plentiful local drinks instead. To return the favor of the meal, invite your colleague out another time. Since many better restaurants are not immediately obvious to the outside observer, ask your colleague or your hotelier for some suggestions.

## Dining in a Private Home

If you are doing business in Argentina, chances are your host may invite you back to dine at his home. "We are very open with foreigners," said one executive. "We don't just hang them out to dry, we take care of them." If an Argentine really takes a liking to you, he will invite you for a Saturday or Sunday afternoon asado, in which case one should prepare to stay the entire day.

Guests should arrive 20 to 30 minutes late for a meal. Although a host may not expect you to bring anything, the hostess will appreciate flowers. Take care to avoid lilies since they represent death. Good quality chocolates, ice cream, or imported liquor also serve as proper hostess gifts. Avoid wine as an overly common gift. And, to stay on the safe side of fashion, it's always better to overdress.

If you are the honored guest, you will be seated to the right of the hostess. As Argentines take great pride in their food traditions, it's best to eat all the food on your plate, while remembering to compliment the hostess for the food. As an honored guest, one can also expect to be the center of attention as everyone will be curious to know what you think about Argentina.

# 20 Socializing

Being social is an essential part of what it is to be Argentine. A separate time slot does not need to be set aside for Argentines to kick back and relax. As such, a visitor will often find cafes packed full in the middle of the day. "We still manage to have fun, even when we're at work," says one 35-year-old manager. When not in the office, Argentines like to stroll down streets arm-in-arm and window shop or drop by a friend's house. "In North America you have to call someone before you come over—can you imagine?!" says one aghast Argentine. Creatures of habit, Argentines tend to stick close to home, and if they leave town for a vacation they usually return to the same place every year. On the weekends, one can usually find Argentines at the park or on the beach lingering over long and leisurely meals, with plenty of time to debate politics or the latest soccer scores.

## Trasnochecer

Argentines are night people. One will find more people on the streets at 3 A.M. than at 3 P.M. The numerous *boliches* (dance bars) usually don't get going until 1 or 2 A.M. and don't stop until 6 or 7 A.M. To stay awake until late into the night, many take naps from 10 P.M. until midnight. Cafes stay open until the wee hours and restaurants don't start filling up until 10 P.M. Most theaters have a *trasnoche* (overnight movie) that runs some time after 1 A.M. For those accustomed to dinner followed by a movie in their homeland, plan on the reverse in Argentina, an 11 P.M. movie followed by dinner.

## Movie Buffs

Argentines are avid movie fans. An active homegrown industry, heavily encouraged by generous government subsidies, has produced movies of international acclaim. Some of best known movies include: *La Historia Official* (The Official Story), directed by Luis Puenzo, which won an Oscar for best foreign film in 1986; *El Hombre Mirando al Sudeste* (Man Facing Southeast), based on Adolfo Bioy Casares' novel *The Invention of Morel*; and the *Kiss of the Spiderwoman* based on the book by Manuel Puig. To pay homage to both the domestic and international movie industry, the beach resort city of Mar del Plata holds an annual film festival that manages to attract regulars such as Sophia Loren, Alain Delon, and Raquel Welch.

## Tango

While Tango music and dance has become all the rage abroad, at home it largely remains an art appreciated by the older generation and tourists. It nevertheless remains omnipresent in Argentine culture. There are few Argentines who don't know all the words to *El dia que me quieras* by Carlos Gardel, also known as the songbird of Buenos Aires. The leading Tango singer during its golden age from

1920 to 1950, Gardel met his death in a tragic airplane accident in 1935.

A tourist will hear Tango on the radio and see it performed in the street. The traditional Tango neighborhoods of San Telmo and La Boca in Buenos Aires are filled with Tango dinner and dance shows, among them the famous *El Viejo Almacén* and *Club del Vino*. For those looking for a more hands-on experience, plenty of local tango salons offer free lessons to beginners.

## Futbol, Futbol y mas Futbol

Soccer, or *futbol*, without a doubt, remains the number one passion of all Argentines. "What do Argentines care about?" said one government employee. "Soccer, soccer, and soccer. If we win the World Cup, then no matter what happens to the economy or in politics, for us, everything's okay."

Buenos Aires possesses the highest density of first division soccer teams in the world and tournaments go on year round. The most important rivalry exists between the upscale River Plate, known as The Millionaires from the ritzy northern district of Barrio Norte, and the Boca Juniors, the team of soccer great Diego Maradona. One can find Boca's stadium, known as *La Bombonera* (the chocolate box), located in the poor immigrant neighborhood of La Boca. Foreigners going there should take care since fans enjoy spitting and urinating on fellow spectators, and the team's *barra bravas* (hooligans) have been convicted of killing fans from rival teams.

## Games People Play

Other major sports include Formula One racing, of which Argentine taxi drivers are amateur aficionados. Sailing is popular in the Rio de la Plata estuary. Many sports relate to the Argentine love of horses. Argentina leads the world in polo with the famous *Campeonato Abierto Argentino de Polo* tournament held in late November. A mix of polo and basketball, *pato* is an uniquely Argentine game played by gauchos as far back as the 16th century. Originally played with a multi-handled leather basket that contained a duck inside, the violent game caused the death and dismemberment of both duck and players. The sport has since become more civilized, and the duck has been replaced by a leather ball. For those who like the "the sport of kings," horse races take place year round.

## A La Playa

During the hot, muggy summer months of January and February, most of the country shuts down and the population heads en masse to the beach. Two resorts in particular become inundated by Porteños—Mar del Plata in the province of Buenos Aires and Punta del Este in Uruguay, where many socialites own exclusive homes. During this time, Argentine newspapers and TV channels relocate to the Atlantic Coast. But unless you want to experience the crowds first hand, avoid the beach until later in the year.

## Basic Spanish Phrases

| English | Argentine Spanish |
| --- | --- |
| Yes | *Sí* |
| No | *No* |
| Good Morning | *Buenos días* |
| Good Afternoon | *Buenas tardes* |
| Good Evening | *Buenos noches* |
| Hello | *Holá* |
| Good-bye | *Chau; Adiós* |
| Please | *Por favor* |
| Thank you | *Gracias* |
| Pleased to meet you | *Encantado* |
| Excuse me | *Perdón* |
| I'm sorry | *Lo siento* |
| My name is___ | *Me llamo___* |
| I don't understand | *No entiendo* |
| See you tomorrow | *Hasta mañana* |

# Correspondence

The order of information on an Argentine mailing address is slightly different than some Westerners will be used to, particularly since the street number follows the street name. A sample address:

Sr. Juan Perez
Editorial Internacional S.A.
Cabello 3791 2 P. "J"
1425 BUENOS AIRES

The titles of Señor, Señora, or any other professional or academic titles are commonly abbreviated. S.A. (Sociedad Anonima) refers to a corporation. Other variations include S.A.I.C. or S.R.L. Note that Argentines do not include "Street" or "Avenue" in the description of the street unless it officially appears as part of its name, such as *Avenida de Mayo*. *P* abbreviates *piso* (floor) and can sometimes be substituted for *Of.*, the abbreviation for office. Place the *codigo postal* (postal code) before the city name. In the case of Buenos Aires, Argentines commonly refer to it in speech and in writing as *Capital Federal*, and often abbreviate it to read *Bs. As* or BA.

Private mail services, kiosks (identified with the sign *Correo Argentino*), and recently privatized official post offices sell postage stamps.

# 23 Useful Telephone Numbers

Argentine country code . . . . . . . . . . . . . . . . . . . . [54]
City Codes
    Buenos Aires . . . . . . . . . . . . . . . . . . . . . . . . . (11)
    Cordoba . . . . . . . . . . . . . . . . . . . . . . . . . . . . (51)
    Mendoza . . . . . . . . . . . . . . . . . . . . . . . . . . . (61)
    Posadas . . . . . . . . . . . . . . . . . . . . . . . . . . . . (752)
    Rosario . . . . . . . . . . . . . . . . . . . . . . . . . . . . (41)
    Santa Fe . . . . . . . . . . . . . . . . . . . . . . . . . . . . (42)
    San Juan . . . . . . . . . . . . . . . . . . . . . . . . . . . . (64)
    San Rafael . . . . . . . . . . . . . . . . . . . . . . . . . . (627)
Assistance Numbers
    International direct dial access . . . . . . . . . . . . . 00
    Information (directory assistance) . . . . . . . . . 110
    International Operator . . . . . . . . . . . . . . . . . . . 000
    International Information . . . . . . . . . . . 953-8000
    Visitor Information (BA) . . . . . . . (11) 4312-2232
    . . . . . . . . . . . . . . . . . . . . . . . . . . . . (11) 4312-6560
    Visitor Information (Córdoba) . . . . . (51) 44-027
    Visitor Information (Mendoza) . . . (61) 24-2800
    Visitor Information (Rosario) . . . . . (41) 24-8382
    Police, fire, or ambulance . . . . . . . . . . . . . . . . 101
    Argentine Chamber of Commerce (11) 4331-8051

Medical Care
    The British Hospital . . . . . . . . . . (11) 4304-1081
    Hospital Italiano . . . . . . . . . . . . . . (11) 4981-5010
Translation services
    Language Source ASS . . . . . . . . (11) 4342-4229
    Interlingua . . . . . . . . . . . . . . . . . . (11) 4342-0161
Courier services
    DHL . . . . . . . . . . . . . . . . . . . . . . . (11) 4331-3217
    FedEx . . . . . . . . . . . . . . . . . . . . . . (11) 4393-6127
    UPS c/o Airway Systems . . . . . . (11) 4347-1000
Car Rentals
    Localiza . . . . . . . . . . . . . . . . . . . . (11) 4375-1611
    AI . . . . . . . . . . . . . . . . . . . . . . . . . (11) 4312-9475
    Hertz . . . . . . . . . . . . . . . . . . . . . . (11) 4312 1317
Airlines
    Aerolineas Argetinas . (11) 4362-5008, 4393-5122
    Aero Perú . . . . . . . . . . . . . . . . . . (11) 4311-6431
    American Airlines . . . . . . . . . . . (11) 4312-3640
       toll-free . . . . . . . . . . . . . . . . . . . (11) 4318-1111
    Austral . . . . . . . . . . . . . . . . . . . . . (11) 4325-0505
    Avianca . . . . . . . . . . . . . . . . . . . . (11) 4394-5990
    British Airways . . . . . . . . . . . . . . (11) 4325-1059
    Canadian Airlines . . . . . . . . . . . (11) 4322-3732
    Iberia . . . . . . . . . . . . . . . . . . . . . . (11) 4327-2739
    Ladeco . . . . . . . . . . . . . . . . . . . . . (11) 4326-9937
    Lan Chile . . . . . . . . . . . . . . . . . . . (11) 4311-5334
    Lapa . . . . . . . . . . . . . . . . . . . . . . . (11) 4819-5272
    Lineas Aereas Paraguayas . . . . . (11) 4393-1000
    Lloyd Aereo Boliviano . . . . . . . . (11) 4326-3595
    Lufthansa . . . . . . . . . . . . . . . . . . (11) 4319-0600
    Pluna . . . . . . . . . . . . . . . . . . . . . . (11) 4342-4420
    Saeta . . . . . . . . . . . . . . . . . . . . . . (11) 4393-1527
    Swissair . . . . . . . . . . . . . . . . . . . . (11) 4319-0000
    TAP . . . . . . . . . . . . . . . . . . . . . . . (11) 4811-0984
    United Airlines . . . . . . . . . . . . . . (11) 4326-9111
    Varig . . . . . . . . . . . . . . . . (11) 4329-9200 or 9201
    Vasp . . . . . . . . . . . . . . . . . . . . . . . (11) 4311-2699

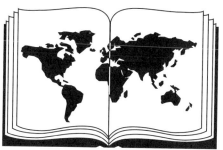

 **Books & Internet Addresses**

**The Invention of Argentina** by Nicolas Shumway. University of California Press, Berkeley, USA, 1991. A Yale professor takes an insightful look at the roots of Argentina's often contradictory and anguished identity, basing his arguments on the country's 19th-century cultural history.

**The Return of Eva Perón** by V. S. Naipaul. Random House, New York, USA, 1974. With the wounds of Argentina's most terrible tragedy in the making, Naipul, with candor and realism, takes a brutally honest look at the schisms that tear at Argentine society and remain applicable to this day.

**Argentina Business: The Portable Encyclopedia for Doing Business in Argentina** 2nd Edition, World Trade Press, Novato, USA, 1998. A comprehensive resource covering 25 key business topics ranging from foreign investment and business law to business culture and trade fairs.

**A Brief History of the Argentines** by Félix Luna. Editorial Planeta, Buenos Aires, Argentina, 1993. Argentina's foremost historian takes a look at the most momentous events to shape Argentina and its people, concluding that the country is moving inexorably toward a strengthened democracy and social egalitarianism.

**Argentina 1516-1987: From Spanish Colonization to Alfonsin** by David Rock. University of California Press, Berkeley and Los Angeles, USA, 1987. Quite simply, the most comprehensive English-language history of the country.

## Web Sites

**Latin American Network Information Center – Argentina**
www.lanic.utexas.edu/la/argentina
**Directory of Argentine Internet Sites**
www.gauchonet.com/index.asp
**Fundacion Invertir—How to do Business in Argentina** (The Internet's best site devoted to business in Argentina.)
www.invertir.com/
**Argentine Wines** (Spanish)
www.argentinewines.com/index.html
**Industrial Guide to Mercosur**
www.nat.com.ar/argwww/indexi.html
**Grippo Argentina Directory**
A search engine for Argentina with links to other search engines. Links are usually in Spanish.
www.grippo.com/
**Ministry of Economy and Public Works**
A search engine with databases categorized by organization, topic, or economic news
www.mecon.ar/
**Trade Leads Online**
A website for companies interested in exporting to or importing from Argentina and Mercosur countries.
www.tradeline.com.ar/